A Suitcase of Dreams

IMMIGRATION STORIES FROM THE SKIRBALL CULTURAL CENTER

Shelly Kale

SKIRBALL CULTURAL CENTER
Los Angeles

Acknowledgments

Special thanks to Dr. Stanley F. Chyet, Assistant to the President at the Skirball Cultural Center, for his careful reading of the text and his excellent suggestions; docents Rachel Levin, Barbara Braun, Elaine Gill, Donna Ritter, and the fifth grade students at La Merced Intermediate in Montebello, California, whose participation in the "Americans and Their Family Stories" program initiated the publication of this book; Glenda Bensussen, Marge Dallis, Janice Shestokes, John Nesbitt and Lynne Gilberg, for their invaluable contributions; and the many families that contributed their family heirlooms to the Project Americana collection.

Copyright © 2001 The Skirball Cultural Center
2701 N. Sepulveda Boulevard
Los Angeles, California 90049
www.skirball.org

At the Skirball Cultural Center:
Uri D. Herscher, *President*
Adele Lander Burke, *Vice President of Museum and Education*
Grace Cohen Grossman, *Senior Curator*
Dorothy Clark, *School Outreach Coordinator*
Marcie Kaufman, *Core Exhibition Manager*
Ina Borenzweig, *Museum Educator*
Stacy Lieberman, *Director of Marketing and Communications*

Publication team:
Shelly Kale, *Managing Editor*
Vickie Sawyer Karten, *Design and Typography*
Anita Keys, *Production Coordinator*

Library of Congress Catalogue Card Number: 2001089941
ISBN: 0-9704295-0-9

Printed in Singapore

The publication of this book was made possible, in part, by a grant from the California Arts Council and an anonymous donor.

Front cover and interior:
Suitcase
Poland, 1930s
Leather and brass
19½ × 29½ × 9½ in. (49.5 × 74.9 × 24.1 cm)
Gift of Allison, Abby, and David Lauterbach in memory of their great-grandmother, Eugenia Lauterbach
HUCSM 31.187

War Orphans with Flags (detail)
Ellis Island, New York, 1921
Courtesy of the American Jewish Joint Distribution Committee Photo Archives

Back cover:
Skirball Cultural Center (detail)
Architects: Moshe Safdie and Associates
Photographer: Timothy Hursley
Courtesy of Timothy Hursley

Students from Kittridge Street Elementary School Participating in the "Americans and Their Family Stories" Program
Skirball Cultural Center, Los Angeles, January 2001
Sheeshooter Photography

Photography:
Susan Einstein: pp. 8, 10, 11 (top), 12, 13, 15, 18 (Italian), 19 (bottom), 22 (top), 24 (left top and bottom), 25 (bottom), 26, 27 (cap and bat), 29 (cap and cereal box); John Reed Forsman: pp. 9 (top), 11 (bottom), 18 (English, Yiddish), 23 (left), 24 (right, bottom), 25 (top), 27 (left); Grant Mudford: pp. 3 (bottom), 16; Bill Aron: 19 (top), 30.

Preface

When I was thirteen years old, my family and I immigrated to the United States and settled in San Jose, California. As a young immigrant, I was scared of what was ahead of me. I didn't have any friends. I couldn't speak the language. I wondered what would happen to my family and me in this very different land. Much to my delight, I was warmly welcomed by my teachers, fellow students, and neighbors.

I have never forgotten that unexpected kindness. It has been my dream to share that welcome feeling with others. By reaching out to you and your families, the Skirball Cultural Center aims to make you feel at home. This is a place that celebrates the democratic values of our country that we all share. Here, by sharing the Jewish people's four-thousand-year-old culture and traditions, we help you understand how important your own culture and its traditions are in American life.

A Suitcase of Dreams tells the stories of Jewish immigrants whose dreams inspired them to change not only their own lives, but also America itself. It offers an important message: by understanding the past, we can create a better future. The Skirball Cultural Center shares this message. After all, the Skirball Museum collects art and artifacts that immigrants throughout the centuries have brought to America. Now, you and future generations can enjoy, study, and learn from them.

It is our hope that this book will help all families in America tell their story.

Every child in America has stories and dreams. What are yours?

Uri D. Herscher

President and Chief Executive Officer
Skirball Cultural Center

Uri D. Herscher as a child and today at the Skirball Cultural Center in Los Angeles.

Introduction

In 1863, President Abraham Lincoln described immigrants as a "source of national wealth and strength." At that time, the United States was a very different place than it is today. There was no space travel, television, or Internet. But something was about to happen that would change our country forever. Between 1880 and 1920, thirty million men, women, and children would leave their homelands from across the oceans and journey to America.

Who were these newcomers—these immigrants? Why did they leave their homes? What did they bring with them? What happened to them when they arrived? How is their story important to America?

In the following pages, you will learn about immigration to America through the experiences of one group of immigrants—the Jewish immigrants, mostly from Eastern Europe. Many of their experiences were shared by other groups of immigrants who came here. What Jewish immigrants brought with them—and what they contributed to America—helps us to understand why all immigrants come here and what they hope to achieve.

People make history, and family stories are part of history. Even now, as you read this book or go to school or play a sport, you are making history. Your story and the story of your family are part of America's story.

When we think of a story, we think of something we read in a book or see on television or in the movies. But objects on display in a museum tell a story, too. In this book, the story of Jewish immigration is told through paintings, photographs, objects, and family treasures at the Skirball Cultural Center in Los Angeles.

Most of these objects and treasures were handed down from generation to generation. They are called heirlooms. The families of the people who used them gave them to the museum. You will meet these families and learn their stories through their heirlooms. Objects that we use in our everyday lives help us tell our family stories and understand our history.

Today, nearly everyone in America is either an immigrant or a descendant of an immigrant. Are President Lincoln's words—written over a century ago—about how important immigrants are to America still true? Let's find out!

"...source of national wealth and strength."
– Abraham Lincoln

This painting, called *Generations/Return*, by Malcah Zeldis, shows how and why the Jewish people immigrated to the United States and to Israel.

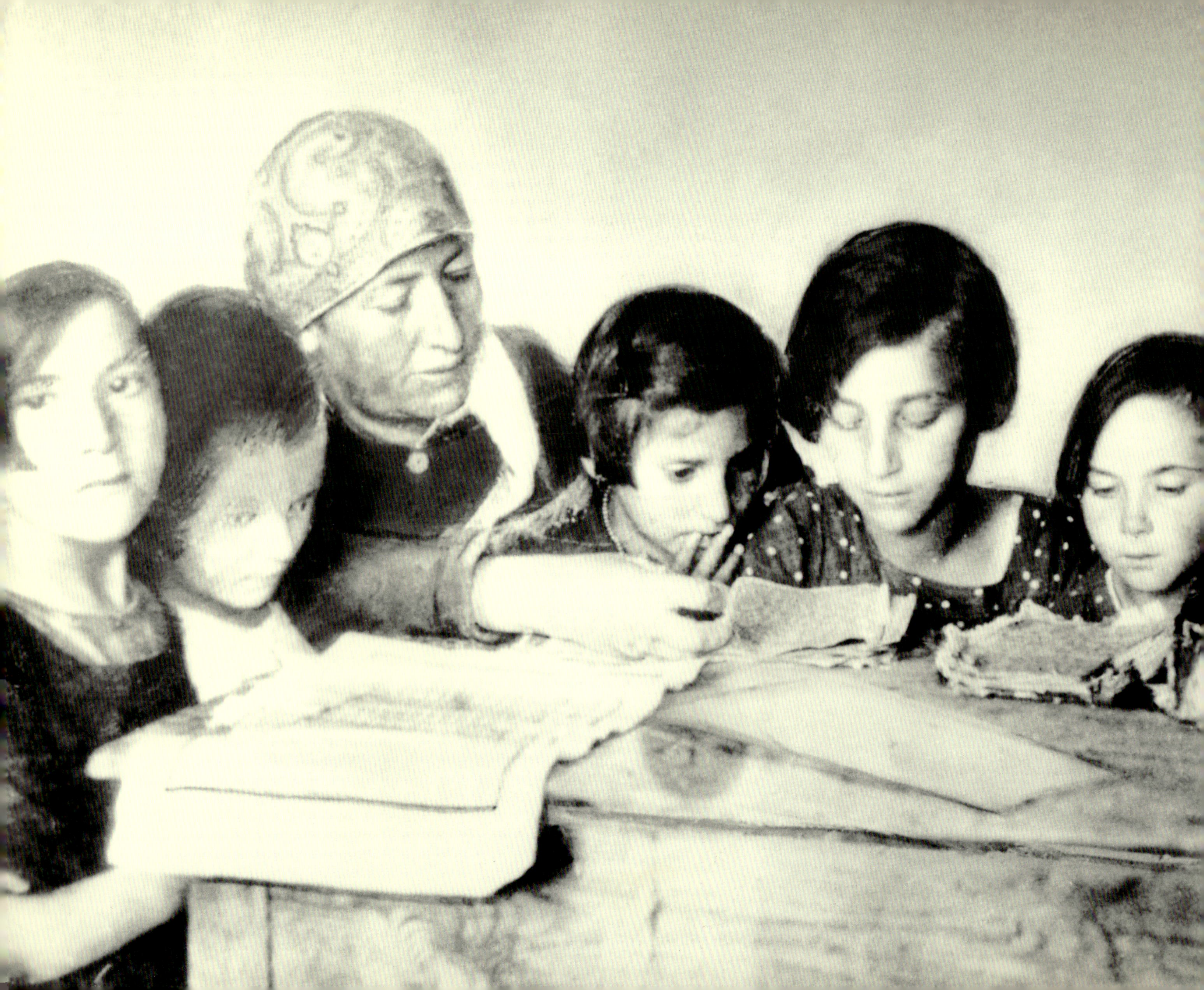

Leaving Home

Imagine you're leaving your homeland in search of a new place to live. You have many questions: Why am I leaving? Where will I go? What should I bring with me? What will my new home be like? Will I be happy there? These questions have been asked by millions of people who have come to live in the United States. But you don't have to move to a new country to understand how it feels to experience the unknown. Maybe you once moved to a new city, neighborhood, or school. How did you feel? Scared? Excited? Sad? Hopeful?

Did someone in your family leave his or her homeland to come to a new place? Who? What is his or her story?

If you were one of the girls in this religious school, you might look forward to moving to a new land, with more modern classrooms and newer books. Or maybe you'd be sad saying goodbye to the only life you knew — your family, friends, school, and neighborhood. Or perhaps, like the Irish who were driven across the Atlantic by famine or the Africans who were brought here as slaves, you did not choose to leave your homeland, but were forced to leave.

These girls are students in a Jewish religious school – a *heder* – in Poland in the mid-1920s.

The artist Peter Krasnow depicted how he felt about leaving his home. He was born in the Ukraine (then part of Russia) in 1887, a time when many Jewish families were victims of pogroms, murderous attacks by violent mobs. Many Jewish people were killed. Others were forced to leave. After Peter immigrated to the United States, he painted this picture of himself and his wife, Rose, leaving their homeland.

In the painting, Rose looks straight ahead, her eyes opened to the future. She looks hopeful. Peter, however, turns to look back at those he is leaving behind. How do you think he feels? How do you think the people who are staying behind feel?

Like Peter and Rose, many immigrants found it hard to balance their dream of making a better life in a new land with their fear of leaving behind everything they had known. The everyday objects they brought with them helped them to remember their homeland as they created new lives.

Seeking a Better Future

The story of Jewish immigration begins long ago. Since ancient times, Jewish people have moved from place to place to get better jobs and to escape war and prejudice. They settled in countries throughout the world—Egypt, Persia, Spain, Italy, France, England, Holland, Germany, Russia, Poland, Greece, even China.

Revan Komaroff and his family left Russia in 1865. Before coming to the United States, the Komaroffs lived in Shanghai, where they helped to build a synagogue—a

The Wanderers by Peter Krasnow.

Revan Komaroff's prayer shawl and bag from China.

Jewish house of prayer and study.

In China, Revan used this prayer shawl and bag for his bar mitzvah — the religious ceremony for thirteen-year-olds that celebrates becoming an adult in the Jewish community. The silk prayer shawl, called a *tallit,* and its bag were made and decorated in China. The Komaroff family kept this tradition from their culture alive — preserving their family story and their heritage.

The Nissim and Jacob families, originally from Iraq, moved to China in the 1800s to work. Years later, in 1951, they moved to San Francisco.

Like many immigrants, the Nissim and Jacob families adapted to their new home in China. In the photograph, the children are posing in front of the Jacob family home in Shanghai. They have come for a surprise party and are dressed up in traditional Chinese clothes.

Zhitomir is a small city in the Ukraine. Jewish families settled there as early as 1792. By the early 1900s, over 30,000 Jewish people lived there.

The Nissim and Jacob children in China in 1935.

"Our factory has been taken over by the government and we have no income anymore. Tomorrow we will try to escape through Turkey. We will have to put our lives in the hands of a smuggler. A whole life I leave behind."

– Farah Yousefzadeh, Iranian Jewish immigrant, 1980

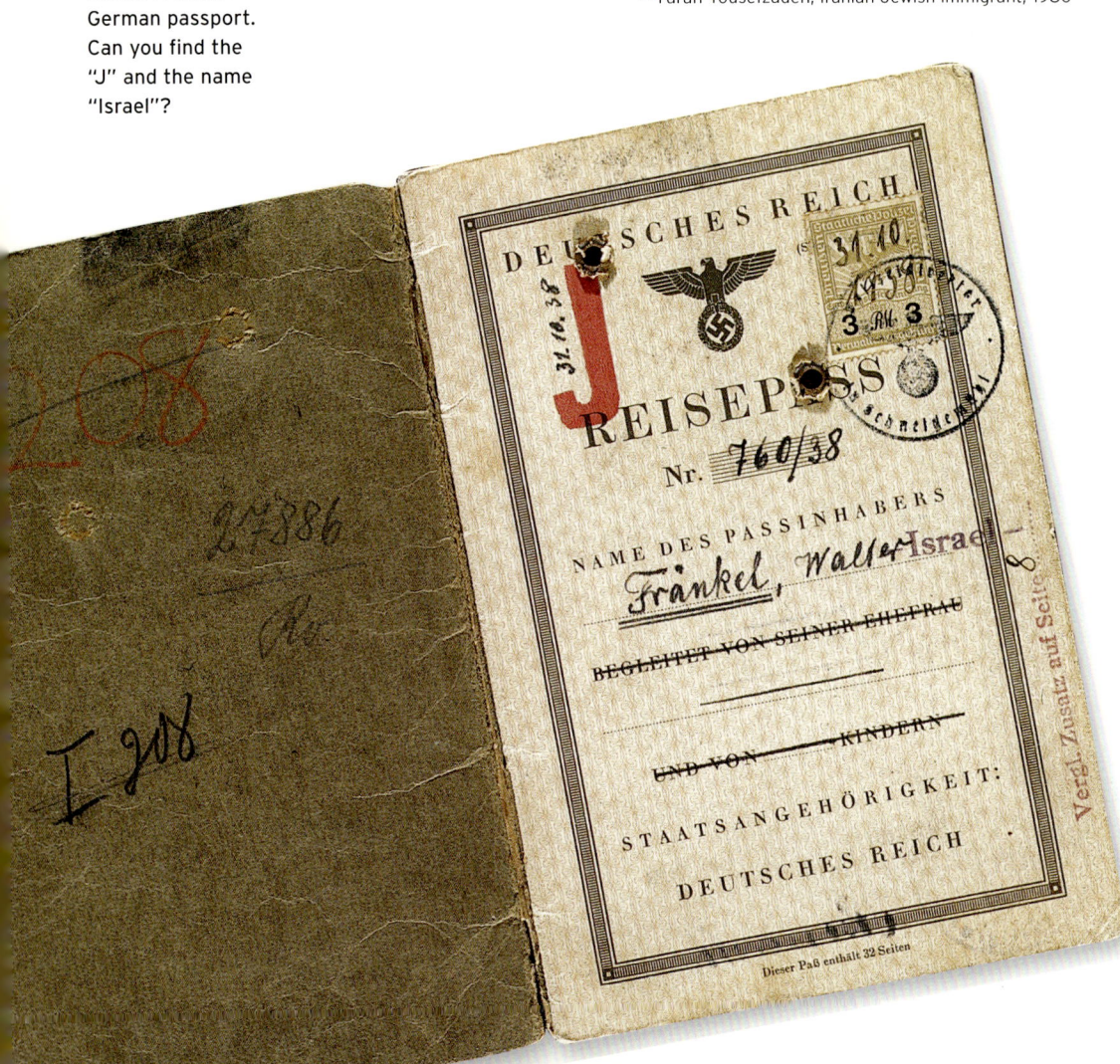

Walter Fränkel's German passport. Can you find the "J" and the name "Israel"?

What can you tell about this Jewish family from Zhitomir? Do they look like they earn enough money to buy the things they need? Why would they want to come to America?

In 1939, Mr. and Mrs. Walter Fränkel left their home in Germany. With this passport, they were able to escape from the German leader Adolf Hitler and his Nazi party. The Nazis' hatred of the Jewish people led to the murder of six million European Jewish men, women, and children by the end of World War II (1939–1945). The Fränkels traveled first to China and then to the United States.

The passports the Nazis gave to Jewish families had the letter "J" on them, for *Jude,* the German word for Jew. The Nazis also added the name "Israel" to each man's name and "Sarah" to each woman's name to further identify them as Jews.

Many immigrants believed that in America they would be free to live as they wished. They could earn more money, and their children could have a good education.

Jewish immigrants had a Yiddish word for America: the *goldeneh medineh* — golden land. In the *goldeneh medineh*, some believed, the streets were paved with gold.

Packing Your Suitcase

What do you take with you to the *goldeneh medineh*? What do you leave behind? Many immigrants brought only a few things — some clothing, a prayer book, pictures of family members they would miss.

A Jewish family in Zhitomir in the early 1900s.

Marcus Jonas was a teenager when he left Germany in the 1870s for California. His father gave him the family shofar to take with him. The shofar is a ram's horn that is blown in the synagogue to announce the beginning of a new Jewish year. For the Jonas family, it was a very special object.

When he arrived in California, Marcus made a special box for the shofar. With this box, he created a New World object for an Old World one. What special family object would you bring with you?

Marcus Jonas's shofar and case.

What are some of the freedoms the United States offered immigrants? How do we enjoy these freedoms today?

RATNER MEDIA AND TECHNOLOGY CENTER
JEWISH EDUCATION CENTER OF CLEVELAND

11

Romanian trunk, with embroidered items.

Thirteen-year-old Goldina Eisenstein Schwartz packed her belongings in this trunk when she left Romania for the United States in 1883. Pictured in the trunk are clothes, table linens, and bedcovers belonging to the Brill family from Romania. In 1905 Aron and Leah Brull (the original spelling of the family name) and their son Harold came to America. Leah was a talented needleworker. She brought these items that she had beautifully embroidered in Romania.

The immigrants packed items they felt would help them to live more comfortably — pillows and blankets for the long voyage to America and objects to use in their new kitchens. Many Jewish immigrants from Eastern Europe brought samovars, which they used to make tea. Why do you think they would bring something so large and heavy?

The immigrants couldn't pack everything they wanted into their suitcases. But they brought other, more important things with them, like hope, confidence, hospitality, love, discipline, and friendship. These values would help them to be successful in their new country. Some even brought objects to remind them of these values.

Trays for sweets were brought to the United States from Greece and Turkey. They were used to serve sweets when welcoming guests to the home. How do you think families who brought sweet trays from their homelands felt about the importance of friends and neighbors?

Before and during World War II, many Jewish immigrants had to leave their

A samovar from Russia.

homes in a hurry and could pack only a few suitcases. Some had to leave in secret.

Marion Stiebel Siciliano was a teenager when she left Germany in April 1938. Her mother told her that they were going on a vacation to Italy, but they were really escaping from the Nazis. Marion was not told where they were going, because there was great danger of being discovered. There was not even time for her to say goodbye to her friends.

Marion packed things she thought she would enjoy on vacation, including her tennis racket and her hand harmonica. Marion's mother brought a typewriter. She hoped she could use it to help earn money for her family in America.

What would you pack in *your* suitcase? What if you had only five minutes to pack? What dreams would you bring with you?

"It was time for us to prepare to leave. We planned to travel at night and spend our days in synagogues. We would take only one piece of luggage, some important papers, and a few photographs tied in a handkerchief."

– Abe Nebrat, Russian Jewish immigrant, 1922

A tray for sweets from Turkey.

Marion Siciliano thought she was going on vacation when she and her family left Germany forever with these belongings.

13

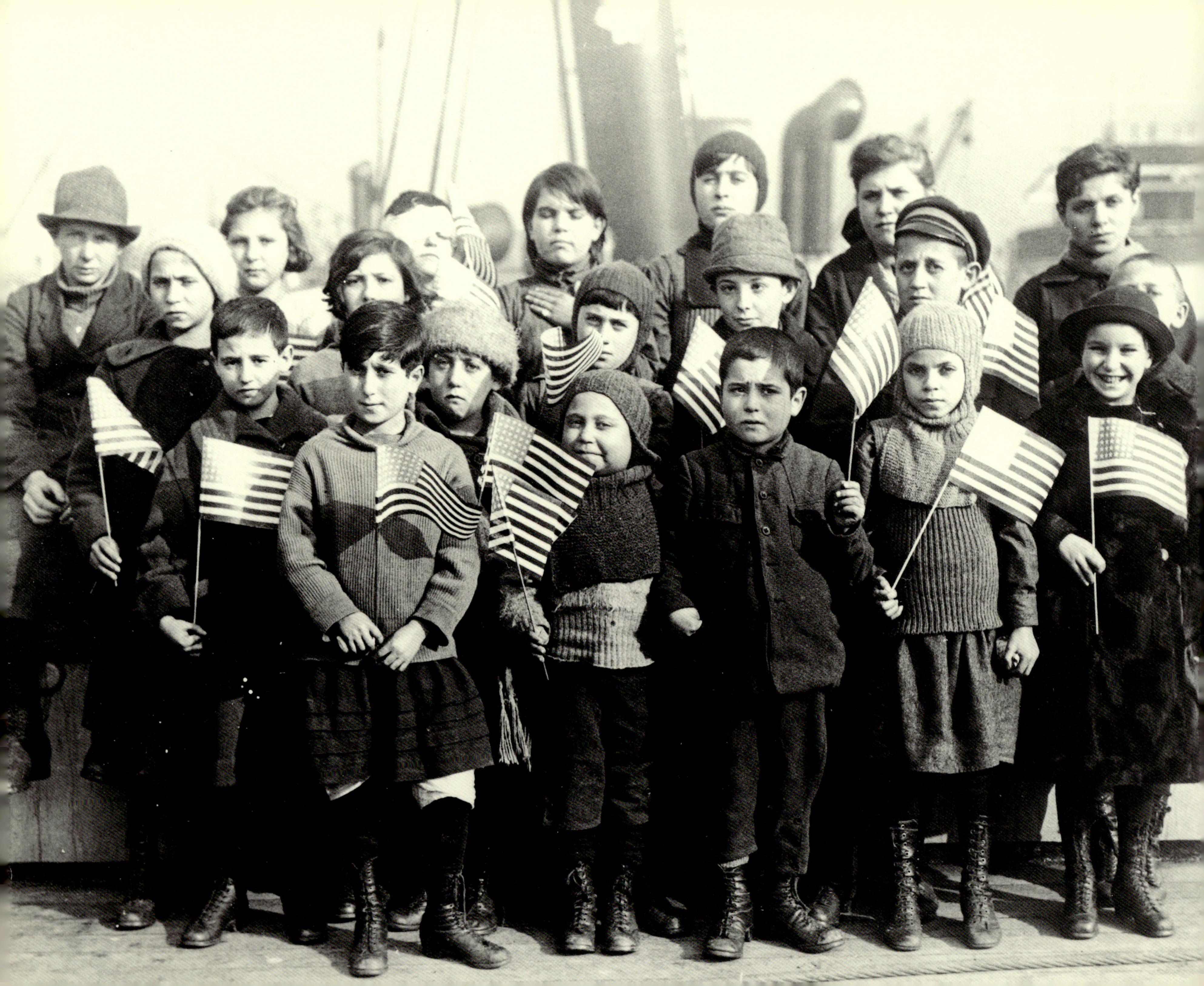

Arriving in America

In the days before airplanes, the journey to the United States was difficult and dangerous. Nearly two and a half million Jewish people were among the thirty million immigrants who crossed the Atlantic Ocean on ships from the 1880s to the 1920s. The voyage over three thousand miles lasted between a few weeks and six months.

Many families could afford to buy only one or two ship tickets. Some sent a child or a few children to join relatives living in America. How would you feel leaving your family behind? Or traveling by yourself to a strange country?

"One evening Papa told the family that he was going on a long journey to a place called America to seek a better life for all of us. Papa said he would send for us as soon as he was settled. Where was America? What would life be like there? When would we see Papa again?"

—Abe Nebrat, Russian Jewish immigrant, 1922

These Jewish war orphans have just arrived in America, the land of liberty and opportunity.

The Journey across the Ocean

Immigrants bought their tickets from the ship companies. Many immigrants were very poor. They could only afford to travel below deck in the steerage section. A steerage ticket cost about $35 — a lot of money in those days!

Before a ship left for America, the ship doctors examined the immigrants to make sure that they were not ill or carrying any disease that could spread to other passengers. The ship companies also filled out a list of everyone on the ship — called a manifest. The manifest included a description of each passenger — his or her age, sex, nationality, and more. The immigrants were now ready to board the ship. Many traveled in the steerage section.

The steerage section was extremely crowded. People often slept on beds stacked one above the other. There was little room to move about. The air was stale. It was dirty. Germs spread easily, and many immigrants got sick.

This is the ship inspection card of Rivke Rosenfeld, who left for the United States from England aboard the *Merion* in April 1914.

This copy of the Statue of Liberty's hand and torch is on display at the Skirball Cultural Center.

What message would you put on the Statue of Liberty for today's immigrants?

"Coming to New York I saw Jell-O for the first time. With the motions of the ship the Jell-O shook and wiggled, so I thought it was alive and was afraid to eat it."

—Mickie Newdorf, Austrian Jewish immigrant, 1938

Welcome!

As ships entered New York harbor, the first thing immigrants saw was the Statue of Liberty. She was, and still is, the symbol of all immigrants' hopes and dreams. She was a gift to the United States from the people of France, who admired the American vision of freedom and liberty.

The American Jewish poet Emma Lazarus hoped to capture the spirit of America's welcome to the immigrants in her poem, *The New Colossus*. The poem won a competition to help raise money for the statue's pedestal. These are its famous last lines:

> Give me your tired, your poor,
> Your huddled masses yearning to breathe free,
> The wretched refuse of your teeming shore.
> Send these, the homeless, tempest-tost to me,
> I lift my lamp beside the golden door!

The First Steps of Freedom

When the immigrants arrived in America, inspection officers examined the first and second class passengers aboard ship. If all went well, they were able to enter the country. Immigrants who had traveled in third class or steerage were brought to the Ellis Island reception center in New York harbor, after it was opened in 1892.

These immigrants are standing on the deck of a ship bound for America. What can you see in their faces as their ship approaches land? Relief? Excitement? Worry? Fear?

In the Great Hall on Ellis Island, immigration inspectors examined thousands of immigrants. Could the newcomers hear and see? Were they sick? Could they read or pass an intelligence test? The examinations took less than five minutes, but they were the most important minutes of the immigrants' lives. If they didn't pass, they had to return to their homeland.

Ellis Island was called both the Island of Hope and the Island of Tears. Can you explain why?

A New Land

Making a new life in America was very difficult. Immigrants had to find a place to live, get a job, and learn a new language and new customs.

"Food Will Win the War" posters were published especially for immigrants and placed in their neighborhoods during World War 1 (1914–1918). The red, white, and blue rainbow and the golden buildings in the background reminded the immigrants of the beauty, promise, and joy of arriving in America.

The posters were published in several different languages — including English, Italian, and Yiddish — so that the immigrants could read them.

These posters asked immigrants to help America by not wasting food.

"I remember riding the subway and thought all of America was underground."

–Sorrell Wayne, Latvian Jewish immigrant, 1940

> "When my mother came here she wondered why Americans were talking to themselves. She learned they were chewing gum."
>
> – Ida Schreiber, about her mother, a Lithuanian Jewish immigrant in 1920

Eventually, most immigrants became citizens. To become a U.S. citizen, you have to pass a test showing that you know American history and government. You must be able to read, write, and speak English. You also must show that you have not broken any laws and swear that you will be loyal to the United States.

Many of today's immigrants arrive by airplane, car, or bus, or even by foot. Their journey may not be as long or dangerous as those who traveled by ship a century ago, but they bring with them the same hopes and dreams for a better life.

Today, immigrants from all around the world come to America. Like the immigrants before them, they are looking for freedom and opportunity. Do you think they will find it?

In 1990, this Russian Jewish family from Odessa arrived at the Los Angeles airport to begin a new life.

What is liberty? Why is it so important?

This certificate granted Reuben Greenspoon his U.S. citizenship on September 8, 1948. His story, with his contribution as an immigrant, is on page 22.

CHINESE • GERMAN • CZECHO-SLOVAKIAN • BRAZIL • SPANISH • JEWISH • SCOTCH • ROUMANIAN • ENGLISH • AUST

"In school the first day, the bell rang for recess. I didn't know what it rang for but all the children left the room so I got up and went home."

– Rose Friedman, Polish Jewish immigrant, 1921

I Am an American!

How do you begin a new life? For immigrants, it wasn't easy. Poor immigrants, many of them Jewish, who settled in New York City, lived in tenements, crowded apartment buildings. In the tenements, many families had to share the same space. Living conditions were bad. Life was very different from the villages and towns across the ocean!

Immigrants worked very hard to support their families. Even children worked. However, through education, job training, and the help of Jewish organizations — together with their own creativity and determination — Jewish immigrants succeeded. They were able to adapt to America and pursue the American dream of a better life.

Education in the Classroom

Just as it is today, education was the passport to success in America. Jewish people have always known the importance of education. For centuries, men, boys, and sometimes girls learned to read and study the Hebrew Bible, or Torah. Many Jewish children, however, were not allowed to attend non-Jewish schools in their homelands.

In the United States, Jewish children and adults could go to school. They learned English — sometimes even at night after long hours of work.

Some immigrant children needed to help their families earn money, so they were taken out of school to work. Others were able to continue their education. Through study and hard work, many immigrants were able to get good jobs.

These students—each from a different country—are standing at the blackboard of a New York City public school classroom in the early 1900s. One girl is not assigned a nationality. Can you find her?

Trial lens set and glasses from Dr. Reuben Greenspoon's optometry office.

As a poor immigrant from Russia, Dr. Reuben Greenspoon went to optometry school in New York City while working nights as a streetcar conductor. In 1935, he moved to Los Angeles and later opened an office in Beverly Hills. He became one of the first optometrists to fit contact lenses in California, and many Hollywood actors wore his lenses.

Immigrant children in a typical American public school classroom from nearly one hundred years ago. What are some differences between this classroom and yours today?

Education in the Home

Children were not the only members of Jewish immigrant families to learn new American ways. In 1895, the Jewish social worker Lillian Wald founded the Henry Street Settlement in New York City. In the Settlement's four model rooms, Jewish immigrants learned how to clean, furnish, and maintain a tenement apartment, and how to prepare foods in the "modern" American kitchen.

The Project Americana Kitchen at the Skirball Cultural Center is an example of a Jewish immigrant kitchen from 1900 to 1920. Some of the objects — like the stove and the ice box — were bought in America. Others were brought by immigrants from their homelands. Using familiar items made learning new ways much easier. Which of these objects are used today in your kitchen?

Lillian Wald, founder of the Henry Street Settlement.

The Project Americana Kitchen at the Skirball Cultural Center.

23

These crate labels from California are from Jewish agricultural businesses.

Carousel animals by master carver Marcus Charles Illions. His carousel works are still enjoyed today.

Occupations

How did Jewish immigrants make a living? What jobs did they do? A few were farmers. They grew crops and lived off the land. Others started businesses related to farming, like shipping fruits and vegetables from place to place.

The older Jewish communities were helpful to Jewish newcomers. They helped them find places to live, health care, and jobs. Many immigrants began new lives in the Jewish neighborhoods. They lived and worked there, finding places in the community where their skills could be used.

Morris Goodman immigrated to the United States from Russia in 1900. He worked in a tenement neighborhood in New York City delivering ice and coal.

Morris Goodman driving his ice wagon around 1928.

These ice cleats and tongs were the tools of his trade. Later, as a partner in the Clermont Ice Co. in Hudson, New York, he cut blocks of ice and brought them to homes and businesses in his ice wagon.

As a youth, Marcus Charles Illions became a wood carver in Vilna, Lithuania. When he arrived in the United States in 1888, he opened his own shop in Coney Island, New York, where there were three amusement parks. He became a master carver of carousel animals. His sons and daughter worked in the shop with him.

Marcus Illions's carved synagogue lions.

Marcus Illions used the same skills he had learned as a carver to make these lively lions. They were used in a synagogue in Brooklyn, New York, to decorate the space where the Torah was kept.

Like immigrants today, many Jewish immigrants, including young women and children, worked in the clothing industry. The beautiful wedding dress in this tailor shop belonged to Etta Einhorn, who married Harry Reinish in 1909. They met in Philadelphia at Harry's father's clothing factory, where Etta worked as a seamstress.

The Project Americana tailor shop. Can you find the Singer sewing machine, the tailor's shears (scissors), the spools of thread, and the iron? Are these tools used today?

When Levi Strauss left his homeland in Bavaria in 1847 to join his brother in New York, he never dreamed that creating a business in America would make him famous. Seeking opportunity, Strauss moved to California, where in 1848, gold had been discovered.

By 1853, the Gold Rush had created opportunities for many people. Levi Strauss saw that the miners needed strong pants to wear while panning for gold. He created some out of denim, the toughest material he could find, and put rivets at the corners to make them strong. They were an instant success.

Strauss set up a shop, Levi Strauss & Co., to sell the jeans, which became known as Levi's. Soon even the cowboys of the American West were wearing them. Today everyone wears jeans!

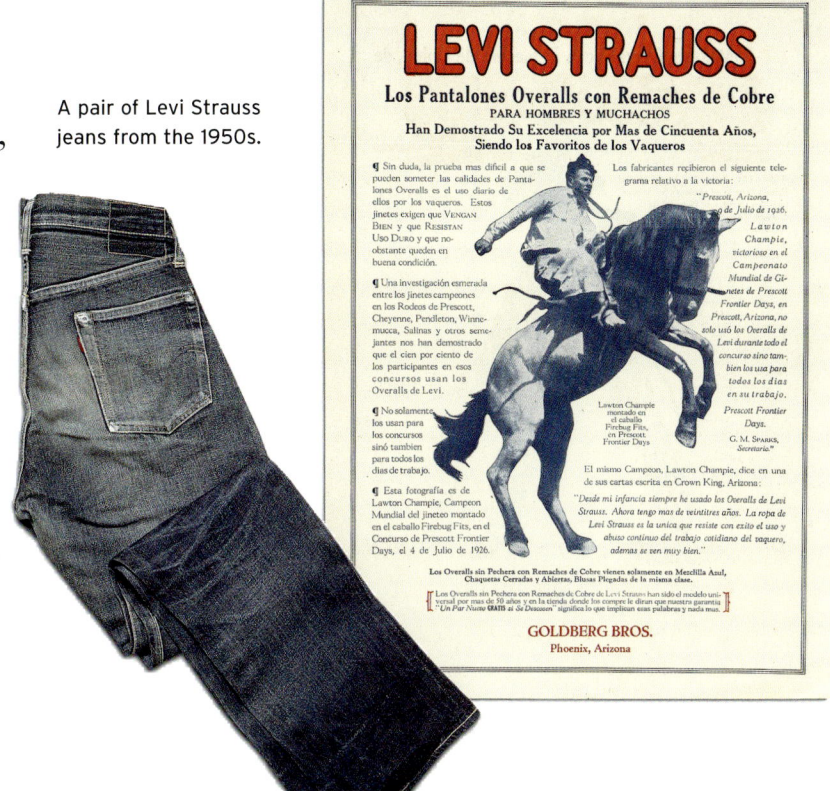

A pair of Levi Strauss jeans from the 1950s.

A real rodeo star helps to tell how strong Levi's jeans are in this Spanish-language ad from the 1920s. Levi Strauss & Co. advertised in many languages, including Chinese and Portuguese, to attract immigrant customers.

This medical license enabled Helene Loewy to practice medicine in her new land.

Helene Loewy had been a doctor in her native land, Germany, but she needed a U.S. license in order to work in America. In 1934, she was granted this license to practice medicine in New York State. She attached her German license to the New York license with red ribbons that she laced through three holes at the top.

Merging Identities

Jewish immigrants were proud to be Americans. They made and used many objects decorated with the symbols of the United States: the Statue of Liberty, the American eagle, the national colors, and the Stars and Stripes of the American flag. In this way, they created a new American Jewish identity for themselves and their families.

What opportunities do you think America offers immigrants today? What jobs are available to today's newly arrived immigrants?

This "V" for Victory banner is an example of American Jewish patriotism.

This "V" for Victory banner, in red, white, and blue was made during World War II (1939–1945) and proudly hung in Jewish homes. On it is a prayer for the U.S. president and vice president written in English, Hebrew, and Yiddish, languages familiar to Jewish Americans.

Many religious objects created in America also combine Jewish tradition and American democratic ideas. This Hanukkah lamp—a traditional symbol of religious freedom used by Jewish people to celebrate the holiday of Hanukkah—was made by Manfred Anson, who immigrated to the United States in 1963.

Anson made the lamp to celebrate the 100th birthday of the Statue of Liberty. He wanted to show how grateful he was for his freedom. He combined the shape of a traditional Hanukkah lamp from Poland with miniature statuettes for candleholders. Each candleholder mentions an important event in Jewish history. With this object, Anson proudly combined Jewish history and ritual with American history and patriotism. What other symbol of America can you see on the lamp?

This cap and bat belonged to Baseball Hall of Famer Henry "Hank" Greenberg. He was born in 1911 in New York City to immigrant Jewish parents from Romania and raised according to traditional Jewish beliefs. He became an American sports hero, but always remembered his religious upbringing.

In 1932, Greenberg's team, the Detroit Tigers, was in a tight pennant race. A pennant game was scheduled to take place on Yom Kippur, the holiest day in the Jewish calendar. Greenberg knew his fans wanted him to play on that day. If he didn't, he might hurt the Tigers' chances of winning the pennant.

When the holy day arrived, Greenberg did not play. The Tigers lost the game, but they did win the American League pennant that year. Greenberg placed his religion's values before his very American job. Do you agree with his decision? What would *you* do?

Manfred Anson's Statue of Liberty Hanukkah lamp.

Baseball Hall of Famer Henry "Hank" Greenberg and his cap and bat.

In what way does your family merge its heritage with its American identity?

Einstein visited the United States in 1930. In 1933, after the Nazis took away his house and all his belongings, he decided to make the United States his new home.

On October 1, 1940, Einstein became a U.S. citizen. His contributions to science earned him the title "father of modern science."

What contributions do *you* hope to make?

Albert Einstein swearing the oath of allegiance to the United States with other immigrants.

Making a Contribution

Even if you are not an immigrant, living in America has made you the person you are today. Because each of us is unique, we each can make a special contribution to our family, our school, our community, our country.

The famous Jewish scientist Albert Einstein was born in Germany in 1879. As a child, he thought of the world as "a great, eternal riddle." He brought this sense of wonder to his studies in mathematics and, later, to his work. In 1922, he won the Nobel Prize in physics.

Ruth Bader Ginsburg was born in Brooklyn, New York, in 1933 to immigrant Jewish parents from central Europe and Russia. As a girl, she took advantage of many opportunities. In high school, she played the cello in the orchestra, was

Ruth Bader Ginsburg at age two and in her robes as a U.S. Supreme Court Justice.

Immigrants helped America become a great nation. What contributions do you think today's immigrants are making?

a cheerleader and baton twirler, edited the school newspaper, and was elected to the honor society.

She continued her education, seeking opportunities that very few women then could. She was one of only nine women admitted to Harvard Law School's class of 1959. As a lawyer and judge, she worked to make sure that men and women were treated equally under the law.

In June 1993, President Bill Clinton appointed her to the United States Supreme Court. She became the first Jewish female Supreme Court Justice in U.S. history.

American Olympic swim champion Lenny Krayzelburg and his family left their home in Odessa, Ukraine, in 1989, when Lenny was fourteen years old.

The Krayzelburgs moved to Los Angeles, where Lenny's parents struggled to earn a living. Lenny had been a promising swimmer before he immigrated, and in America, he worked hard to learn English and keep up with his swimming.

In 1995, Lenny Krayzelburg became an American citizen. He made the U.S. Olympic swim team, and in October 2000, when he was twenty-four, he won three gold medals at the Olympics in Sydney, Australia. Afterward, he told reporters that in America anything is possible. Do you agree?

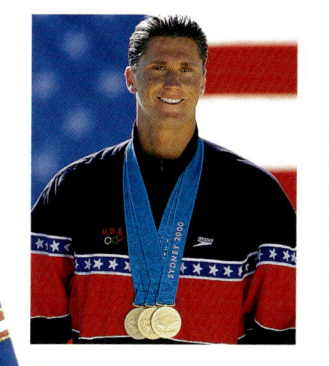

Lenny Krayzelburg wearing his U.S. Olympic gold medals and with "Tony the Tiger" on a box of popular cereal; one of his Olympic team swim caps.

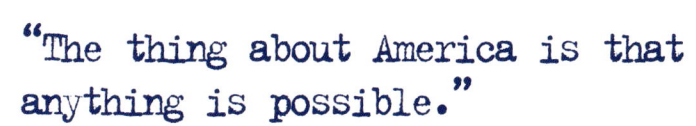

"The thing about America is that anything is possible."

—Lenny Krayzelburg, Russian Jewish immigrant, 2000

29

Conclusion

Just as America changed immigrants, immigrants changed America. Immigrants helped build America's bridges, railroads, skyscrapers, canals, and highways. They contributed to many important aspects of American life. They worked hard!

A century ago, America was known as a "melting pot." People with different customs and nationalities "melted" into one community. Today we have other ways of describing the United States. Our America is a "tapestry," with many different colored threads woven into one fabric. It is a "nation of nations," with people from different nations coming together to form one nation. How would *you* describe America?

Immigrants enrich our lives in many ways — from the foods we eat (like pizza from Italy, tamales from Central America, and falafel from the Middle East) to the words we use (like the Hindi-Chinese word "pajamas" from India). Can you think of other ways that immigrants have made a difference in your life?

Today we are in a new era of immigration. Nine hundred thousand immigrants arrive in the United States each year. They come from Asia, Africa, the Caribbean, Latin America, and many other lands.

More Americans today were born in other countries than at any other time in U.S. history. Two of every ten American schoolchildren have at least one parent who was not born here. How can we help them become Americans?

The historian Oscar Handlin said, "Once I thought to write a history of the immigrants to America. Then I discovered that the immigrants *were* American history."

"I discovered . . . immigrants *were* American history."

– historian Oscar Handlin

A Russian Jewish immigrant arriving in Los Angeles.

Glossary

Adapt. To change something so that it becomes appropriate; to adjust. *The immigrants adapted to their new lives in America.*

Ancestor. The people in our family who came before us, such as our grandparents or great-grandparents (from a Latin word meaning "to go before"). *All of us have ancestors who came to America from different lands.*

Contribution. What you give or do that helps make things happen. *Immigrants make many contributions to American society.*

Culture. The customs and ways of living of a people or a nation. *Our country is made up of many different cultures from all over the world.*

Custom. An accepted way of doing things. *The customs of many countries are practiced in the United States.*

Descendant. The offspring, or future children, of a family, such as a child, grandchild, or great-grandchild. *You are the descendant of an immigrant.*

Generation. All the people who were born around the same time. *Your grandparents passed down your family's story to your parent's generation; they are passing it down to your generation.*

Goldeneh Medineh. "Golden land," the Yiddish name given to America by the Jewish immigrants from Eastern Europe. *The immigrants believed that America was a goldeneh medineh, a rich country, whose streets were paved with gold.*

Heirloom. A family object handed down from generation to generation, such as a photograph, jewelry, furniture, book, or picture. *Heirlooms help to tell our family stories.*

Heritage. The traditions, skills, and culture of a people handed down from one generation to the next. *Freedom is our country's most precious heritage.*

Immigrant. Someone who moves permanently from one country to another. *Between 1880 and 1920, thirty million immigrants came to America.*

Liberty. The condition of being free. *In the United States people have liberty to practice any religion.*

Opportunity. A chance. *Education gave the immigrants and their families an opportunity to succeed in America.*

Passport. A document that allows people to leave their country and travel to another one. *The Jewish families that received passports from the Nazis were able to escape Nazi Germany before and during World War II.*

Pogroms. Attacks against Jews by violent mobs, often organized by governments a century ago. *Many Jewish homes and businesses were robbed and burned and many Jewish people were killed in the pogroms of Eastern Europe in the 1880s.*

Ritual. A system of regularly followed ceremonies. *Blowing the shofar in synagogue is part of the ritual of prayer at the Jewish new year.*

Steerage. The section of a ship for the immigrant passengers who bought the least expensive tickets. Often it is located near the back or the "steering" mechanism of the ship. *There was not much room to move around in the steerage section of the ship, where conditions were very bad.*

Tenement. An apartment building with many small units, often in the poor section of a city. *As the immigrant families began to earn money, they left the tenements and moved to better neighborhoods.*

Tradition. The handing down of customs, beliefs, opinions, stories, and so on from parents to their children. *Becoming bar mitzvah is a Jewish tradition.*

List of Illustrations

To learn more about immigration and the American Jewish experience, visit our website at www.skirball.org or come to the Skirball Cultural Center in Los Angeles. We look forward to your visit!

Page 3
Uri Herscher
Israel (the Mediterranean shore), 1945
Photographer: Joseph Herscher
Courtesy of Uri Herscher

Uri Herscher at the Skirball Cultural Center (detail)
Los Angeles, 1996
Photographer: Grant Mudford
Courtesy of Grant Mudford

Page 4, Interior and back cover
Generations/Return (details)
Malcah Zeldis (b. 1931); New York, 1985
Oil on masonite; 36 × 48 in (88.9 × 122 cm)
Gift of Marian and Donald DeWitt
HUCSM 41.432

Pages 6–7
Girls' Kheyder in Laskarzew
Photographer: Alter Kacyzne
Courtesy of YIVO, Raphael Abramovitch Collection

Page 8
The Wanderers
Peter Krasnow; Los Angeles, 1926
Oil on canvas; 49½ × 32¼ in. (125.7 × 81.9 cm)
Gift of Mr. and Mrs. Peter Krasnow
HUCSM 41.289

Page 9
Prayer Shawl and Bag
Shanghai, China, 1904
Silk, embroidered with silk thread
Bag: 8½ × 11 in. (22 × 28.5 cm)
Shawl: 84 × 29½ in. (213 × 75 cm)
Gift of Mr. and Mrs. Revan Komaroff
HUCSM 46.72a,b

Nissim and Jacob Family Children at a Surprise Party for the Donor's Father in Front of the Family House
Shanghai, China, July 16, 1935
Courtesy of Rose Jacob Horowitz

Page 10
Passport
Germany, 1938
Printed paper and ink; 6½ × 4¼ in. (16.5 × 11.3 cm) open
Gift of Susanne Kester; HUCSM 16.53

Page 11
Family Portrait (detail)
Zhitomir, Russia, early 20th century
Photograph on board; 5¾ × 7 in. (14.5 × 17.8 cm)
HUCSM 68.377b

Shofar and Case
Maker: Marcus Jonas
Oakland, California, ca. 1870
Wood and ram's horn
Case: 3¼ × 16½ × 7 in. (8.3 × 41.9 × 17.8 cm)
Shofar: 2 × 13 × 6 in. (5.1 × 33 × 15.7 cm)
Gift of Mrs. Felix Jonas; HUCSM 52.36a,b

Page 12
Trunk; Clothes and Textiles
Romania, ca. 1890; ca. 1900
Trunk: Gift of Brenda Grossman Spivack in memory of Goldina Eisenstein Schwartz
Clothes and textiles: Gift of Harold Brill and Regina Starr Brill

Samovar
St. Petersburg, Russia, 1847
Brass and wood; 28½ × 11½ × 13½ in. (72.4 × 29.2 × 34.3 cm)
Gift of Kate Gordon Shapiro in loving memory of her mother, Dena Rose Geller Gordon
HUCSM 14.51

Page 13
Tavla de Dulsé
Izmir, Turkey, 1920s
Silver, cast, die-stamped and pierced
Container: 9⅝ × 5¼ in. diam. (24.4 × 13.5 cm)
Dishes: 1¾ × 6 in. diam. (4.5 × 15.2 cm)
Museum purchase with funds provided by the Maurice Amado Foundation at the behest of the Tarica Family; HUCSM 14.357a–o

Suitcases, Tennis Racket and Press, Hand Harmonica and Case, Typewriter
Germany, 1930s
Gift of Marion Stiebel Siciliano; HUCSM 31.97, 31.99, 31.53, 31.93a-d, 31.54

Page 14
War Orphans with Flags
Ellis Island, New York, 1921
Courtesy of the American Jewish Joint Distribution Committee Photo Archives

Page 15
Ship's Inspection Card
England, 1914
Paper, printed; ink; 4 × 5½ in. (10.2 × 14 cm)
Gift of Anne Rosenfeld Berg; HUCSM 19a.88

Page 16
Statue of Liberty Torch
Photographer: Grant Mudford
Skirball Cultural Center, Los Angeles
Courtesy of Grant Mudford

Page 17
Immigrants on a Ship's Deck (detail)
July 24, 1915; SS Prince Fredrick Wilhelm
© CORBIS/Bettmann

Page 18
Food Will Win the War
Maker: Charles Edward Chambers (1883–1941)
United States, ca. 1918
Color lithograph; 30 × 20 in. (76.2 × 50.8 cm)
English version: Museum purchase with funds provided by the Lee Kalsman Project Americana Acquisition Fund; HUCSM 66.2729. Yiddish version: Gift of Dr. and Mrs. Boris Catz; HUCSM 66a.106. Italian version: Museum purchase with funds provided by the Lee Kalsman Project Americana Acquisition Fund; HUCSM 66.2769

Page 19
Certificate of Naturalization
Dated September 8, 1948
8 × 10 in. (20.3 × 25.5 cm)
Gift of Dr. Morton Greenspoon; HUCSM 19a.170

Twins from Odessa (detail)
Photographer: Bill Aron
Los Angeles International Airport, 1990
Courtesy of Bill Aron

Pages 20–21
Children of Different Nationalities
ca. 1900
© CORBIS/Bettmann

Page 22
Trial Lens Set and Glasses
New York City, N.Y., 1914
Wood, metal, and glass; set: 20¼ × 11½ × 1¾ in. (51.4 × 29.2 × 4.4 cm); glasses: 5⅞ × 3¾ × 1⅝ in. (14.9 × 9.5 × 4.2 cm); Gift of Dr. and Mrs. Morton Greenspoon; HUCSM 70.255, 70.252

Elementary School Classroom (detail)
Early 1900s
© CORBIS/Bettmann

Page 23
Project Americana Kitchen (detail)
Gifts of family heirlooms and museum purchases

Lillian Wald
New York, 1893
Courtesy of Visiting Nurse Service of New York

Page 24
Chickie Brand Crate Label
San Francisco, California, early 20th century
Printed paper; 9⅞ × 10 in. (24.8 × 25.3 cm)
Museum purchase with Project Americana Acquisitions Funds
HUCSM 69.74

Queen Esther Brand Crate Label
Maker: Yorba Linda Orange Growers Association
Orange County, California, early 20th century
Printed paper; 10 × 11 in. (25.3 × 27.9 cm)
Museum purchase with funds provided by the Lee Kalsman Project Americana Acquisition Fund; HUCSM 69.285

L-Z Brand Apples Crate Label
San Francisco, California, early 20th century
Printed paper; 9 1/16 × 10 9/16 in. (23 × 26.7 cm)
Museum purchase with funds provided by the Lee Kalsman Project Americana Acquisition Fund; HUCSM 69.283

Ice Cleats and Tongs
New York, ca. 1915
Cleats: leather and iron; 4½ × 4¼ × 8 in. (individual) (11.3 × 10.8 × 20.3 cm)
Tongs: iron, painted; 14½ × 8¾ × 4¾ in. (36.8 × 22.3 × 12 cm)
Gift of the children of Morris Goodman
HUCSM 70.64a,b, 70.65

Morris Goodman
Hudson, New York, ca. 1928
Gift of the children of Morris Goodman

Marcus Illions Carousel Works
Coney Island, New York, ca. 1920
Courtesy of Barney Illions

Synagogue Lions
Maker: Marcus Charles Illions (1865–1949)
Brooklyn, New York, early 20th century
Wood, carved and painted, and glass
20 × 26½ × 3¾ in. (50.8 × 67.3 × 9.5 cm)
Museum purchase with Project Americana Acquisition Funds provided by Irving and Lee Kalsman, Peachy and Mark Levy, and Gerald M. and Carolyn Z. Bronstein; HUCSM 30.13a,b

Page 25
Project Americana Tailor Shop
Gifts of family heirlooms and museum purchases
Wedding dress: HUCSM 9.19

Pair of 501® Jeans
San Francisco, California, 1950s
Cotton denim and copper rivets
On loan from Levi Strauss & Co. Archives, San Francisco

Advertisement in Spanish for Levi Strauss & Co.
San Francisco, California, 1920s
Printed paper; 10⅞ × 8 in. (27.6 × 20.3 cm)
Gift of Levi Strauss & Co. Archives, San Francisco; HUCSM 69.354

Page 26
Medical License
New York City, N.Y., dated December 12, 1934
Printed paper, ink, ribbon, and photograph
10½ × 5½ in. (29.7 × 14 cm)
Gift of Mr. and Mrs. George M. Liss
HUCSM 19a.180

"V" for Victory Prayer
United States, 1941–1945
Rayon and wood; 13 3/16 × 10 in. (33.4 × 22.4 cm)
Gift of Rabbi and Mrs. Alfred Wolf
HUCSM 45a.24

Page 27
Statue of Liberty Hanukkah Lamp
Maker: Manfred Anson (b. 1922); New Jersey, 1985
Brass, cast; 23 × 16½ in. (58.4 × 41.9 cm)
Museum purchase with Project Americana funds provided by Peachy and Mark Levy; HUCSM 27.154

Hank Greenberg at the Stadium
Detroit, Michigan, 1934
14 × 11 in. (35.6 × 28 cm)
Gift of Mrs. Hank Greenberg; HUCSM 68.283

Detroit Tiger Cap
Tim McAuliffe
Boston, Massachusetts, 1940s
Wool and twill polyester; 5 × 11 × 7 in. diam. (12.7 × 27.9 × 17.8 cm)
Gift of Mrs. Hank Greenberg; HUCSM 70.187

Baseball Bat
United States of America, dated July 10, 1984
Wood and metal; 34 × 2½ in. diam. (86.4 × 6.3 cm)
Gift of Mrs. Hank Greenberg; HUCSM 29.288

Page 28
Einstein Taking the Oath of Citizenship
October 1, 1940
Courtesy of AP/WIDE WORLD PHOTOS

Associate Justice Ruth Bader Ginsburg, age 3
Photographer unknown
Collection, The Supreme Court Historical Society
Courtesy of the Office of the Curator of the United States Supreme Court

Associate Justice Ruth Bader Ginsburg
Photographed by Richard Strauss, Smithsonian Institution Collection,
The Supreme Court Historical Society

Page 29
Lenny Krayzelburg's U.S. Olympic Swim Team Cap
Maker: Speedo
United States of America, 2000
Silicone, printed; 8 × 9½ in. irregular (20.3 × 24 cm)
Gift of Lenny Krayzelburg: In honor of my parents Oleg and Yelena for all the support they have given me.
Courtesy of Speedo; HUCSM 77.24

Lenny Krayzelburg
Courtesy of Speedo

Kellogg's Frosted Flakes Box Featuring Lenny Krayzelburg
Maker: ® Kellogg Company
United States of America, © 2000
Cardboard, printed; 12¼ × 7¾ × 2¾ in. (31.1 × 19.7 × 7 cm)
Gift of Dr. and Mrs. Mark Kaufman; HUCSM 77.25
KELLOGG'S FROSTED FLAKES is a trademark of Kellogg Company. All rights reserved. Used with permission.

Page 30
Just Arrived
Photographer: Bill Aron
Los Angeles International Airport, 1990
Courtesy of Bill Aron